GAO

Testimony
Before the Committee on Commerce, Science, and Transportation and the Committee on Homeland Security and Governmental Affairs, U.S. Senate

For Release on Delivery
Expected at 2:30 p.m. EST
Thursday, March 7th, 2013

CYBERSECURITY

A Better Defined and Implemented National Strategy Is Needed to Address Persistent Challenges

Statement of Gregory C. Wilshusen, Director
Information Security Issues

GAO
Accountability * Integrity * Reliability

GAO-13-462T

March 7, 2013

CYBERSECURITY

A Better Defined and Implemented National Strategy Is Needed to Address Persistent Challenges

Highlights of GAO-13-462T, a testimony before the Committee on Commerce, Science, and Transportation, and the Committee on Homeland Security and Governmental Affairs, U.S. Senate

G A O
Accountability * Integrity * Reliability

Highlights

Why GAO Did This Study

Federal government agencies and the nation's critical infrastructures have become increasingly dependent on computerized information systems and electronic data to carry out their operations. While creating significant benefits, this can also introduce vulnerabilities to cyber-threats. Pervasive cyber attacks against the United States could have a serious impact on national security, the economy, and public health and safety. The number of reported cyber incidents has continued to rise, resulting in data theft, economic loss, and privacy breaches. Federal law and policy assign various entities responsibilities for securing federal information systems and protecting critical infrastructures. GAO has designated federal information security as a high-risk area since 1997 and in 2003 expanded this to include cyber critical infrastructure protection.

GAO was asked to testify on its recent report on challenges facing the government in effectively implementing cybersecurity and the extent to which the national cybersecurity strategy includes desirable characteristics of a national strategy. In preparing this statement, GAO relied on the report, as well as related previous work.

What GAO Recommends

In its report, GAO recommended that an integrated national strategy be developed that includes milestones and performance measures; costs and resources; and a clear definition of roles and responsibilities. It also stated that Congress should consider clarifying federal cybersecurity oversight roles through legislation.

View GAO-13-462T. For more information, contact Gregory C. Wilshusen at (202) 512-6244 or wilshuseng@gao.gov, or Dr. Nabajyoti Barkakati at (202) 512-4499 or barkakatin@gao.gov.

What GAO Found

The federal government continues to face challenges in a number of key areas in effectively implementing cybersecurity; these challenge areas include the following, among others:

- **Designing and implementing risk-based cybersecurity programs at federal agencies.** Shortcomings persist in assessing risks, developing and implementing security programs, and monitoring results at federal agencies. This is due in part to the fact that agencies have not fully implemented information security programs, resulting in reduced assurance that controls are in place and operating as intended to protect their information resources.
- **Establishing and identifying standards for critical infrastructures.** Agencies with responsibilities for critical infrastructure have not yet identified cybersecurity guidance widely used in their respective sectors. Moreover, critical infrastructure sectors vary in the extent to which they are required by law or regulation to comply with specific cybersecurity requirements.
- **Detecting, responding to, and mitigating cyber incidents.** Sharing information among federal agencies and key private-sector entities remains a challenge, due to, for example, the lack of a centralized information-sharing system. In addition, the Department of Homeland Security (DHS) has yet to fully develop a capability for predictive analysis of cyber threats.

The federal cybersecurity strategy has evolved over the past decade, with the issuance of several strategy documents and other initiatives that address aspects of these challenge areas. However, there is no overarching national cybersecurity strategy that synthesizes these documents or comprehensively describes the current strategy. In addition, the government's existing strategy documents do not always incorporate key desirable characteristics GAO has identified that can enhance the usefulness of national strategies. Specifically, while existing strategy documents have included elements of these characteristics—such as setting goals and subordinate objectives—they have generally lacked other key elements. These include milestones and performance measures to gauge results; costs of implementing the strategy and sources and types of resources needed; and a clear definition of the roles and responsibilities of federal entities. For example, although federal law assigns the Office of Management and Budget (OMB) responsibility for oversight of federal government information security, OMB recently transferred several of these responsibilities to DHS. This decision may have had practical benefits, such as leveraging additional resources and expertise, but it remains unclear how OMB and DHS are to share oversight of individual departments and agencies. Additional legislation could clarify these responsibilities. Further, without an integrated strategy that includes key characteristics, the federal government will be hindered in making further progress in addressing cybersecurity challenges.

Contents

United States Government Accountability Office
Washington, DC 20548

Chairmen Rockefeller and Carper, Ranking Members Thune and Coburn, and Members of the Committees:

Thank you for the opportunity to testify at today's hearing on the cybersecurity partnership between the private sector and our government.

As you know, with the advance of computer technology, federal agencies and our nation's critical infrastructures—such as the electricity grid, water supply, telecommunications, and emergency services—have become increasingly dependent on computerized information systems and electronic data to carry out operations and process, maintain, and report essential information. While bringing significant benefits, this dependency can also create vulnerabilities to cyber-based threats. Pervasive and sustained cyber attacks against the United States could have a potentially serious impact on federal and nonfederal systems and operations. Underscoring the importance of this issue, we have designated federal information security as a high-risk area since 1997 and in 2003 expanded this area to include protecting computerized systems supporting our nation's critical infrastructure.[1]

Federal law and policy call for a risk-based approach to managing cybersecurity within the government and also specify activities to enhance the cybersecurity of public and private infrastructures that are essential to national security, economic security, and public health and safety. Over the last 12 years, the federal government has developed a number of strategies and plans for addressing cybersecurity based on this legal framework, including the *National Strategy to Secure Cyberspace*, issued in February 2003, and subsequent plans and strategies that address specific sectors, issues, and revised priorities.

In my testimony today, I will summarize (1) several challenges faced by the federal government in effectively implementing cybersecurity, including complying with the Federal Information Security Management Act, and (2) the extent to which the national cybersecurity strategy includes key desirable characteristics of effective strategies. My statement is based on our recently released report examining the federal

---

[1]See most recently, GAO, *High-Risk Series: An Update*, GAO-13-283 (Washington, D.C.: Feb. 14, 2013).

government's cybersecurity strategies and the status of federal efforts to address challenges in implementing cybersecurity,[2] as well as other previous work in this area. (Please see app. I for a list of related GAO products.)

The work on which this statement is based was conducted in accordance with generally accepted government auditing standards. Those standards require that we plan and perform audits to obtain sufficient, appropriate evidence to provide a reasonable basis for our findings and conclusions based on our audit objectives. We believe that the evidence obtained provided a reasonable basis for our findings and conclusions based on our audit objectives.

Background

Threats to systems supporting critical infrastructure and federal information systems are evolving and growing. Advanced persistent threats—where adversaries possess sophisticated levels of expertise and significant resources to pursue their objectives repeatedly over an extended period of time—pose increasing risks. In 2009, the President declared the cyber threat to be "[o]ne of the most serious economic and national security challenges we face as a nation" and stated that "America's economic prosperity in the 21st century will depend on cybersecurity."[3] The Director of National Intelligence has also warned of the increasing globalization of cyber attacks, including those carried out by foreign militaries or organized international crime. In January 2012, he testified that such threats pose a critical national and economic security concern.[4] To further highlight the importance of the threat, on October 11, 2012, the Secretary of Defense stated that the collective result of attacks

---

[2]GAO, *Cybersecurity: National Strategy, Roles, and Responsibilities Need to Be Better Defined and More Effectively Implemented,* GAO-13-187 (Feb. 14, 2003).

[3]President Barack Obama, "Remarks by the President on Securing Our Nation's Cyber Infrastructure" (Washington, D.C.: May 29, 2009).

[4]James R. Clapper, Director of National Intelligence, "Unclassified Statement for the Record on the Worldwide Threat Assessment of the US Intelligence Community for the Senate Select Committee on Intelligence" (January 31, 2012).

on our nation's critical infrastructure could be "a cyber Pearl Harbor; an attack that would cause physical destruction and the loss of life."[5]

The evolving array of cyber-based threats facing the nation pose threats to national security, commerce and intellectual property, and individuals. These threats can be unintentional or intentional. Unintentional threats can be caused by software upgrades or defective equipment that inadvertently disrupt systems. Intentional threats include both targeted and untargeted attacks from a variety of sources. These sources include business competitors, corrupt employees, criminal groups, hackers, and foreign nations engaged in espionage and information warfare. Such threat sources vary in terms of the types and capabilities of the actors, their willingness to act, and their motives. Table 1 shows common sources of adversarial cybersecurity threats.

Table 1: Sources of Adversarial Threats to Cybersecurity

Threat source	Description
Bot-network operators	Bot-network operators use a network, or bot-net, of compromised, remotely controlled systems to coordinate attacks and to distribute phishing schemes, spam, and malware attacks. The services of these networks are sometimes made available on underground markets (e.g., purchasing a denial-of-service attack or services to relay spam or phishing attacks).
Business competitors	Companies that compete against or do business with a target company may seek to obtain sensitive information to improve their competitive advantage in various areas, such as pricing, manufacturing, product development, and contracting.
Criminal groups	Criminal groups seek to attack systems for monetary gain. Specifically, organized criminal groups use spam, phishing, and spyware/malware to commit identity theft, online fraud, and computer extortion.
Hackers	Hackers break into networks for the thrill of the challenge, bragging rights in the hacker community, revenge, stalking, monetary gain, and political activism, among other reasons. While gaining unauthorized access once required a fair amount of skill or computer knowledge, hackers can now download attack scripts and protocols from the Internet and launch them against victim sites. Thus, while attack tools have become more sophisticated, they have also become easier to use. According to the Central Intelligence Agency, the large majority of hackers do not have the requisite expertise to threaten difficult targets such as critical U.S. networks. Nevertheless, the worldwide population of hackers poses a relatively high threat of an isolated or brief disruption causing serious damage.
Insiders	The disgruntled organization insider is a principal source of computer crime. Insiders may not need a great deal of knowledge about computer intrusions because their knowledge of a target system often allows them to gain unrestricted access to cause damage to the system or to steal system data. The insider threat includes contractors hired by the organization, as well as careless or poorly trained employees who may inadvertently introduce malware into systems.

[5]Secretary of Defense Leon E. Panetta, "Remarks by Secretary Panetta on Cybersecurity to the Business Executives for National Security, New York City" (New York, N.Y.: Oct. 11, 2012).

Threat source	Description
International corporate spies	International corporate spies pose a threat to the United States through their ability to conduct economic and industrial espionage[a] and large-scale monetary theft and to hire or develop hacker talent.
Nations	Nations use cyber tools as part of their information-gathering and espionage activities. In addition, several nations are aggressively working to develop information warfare doctrine, programs, and capabilities. Such capabilities enable a single entity to have a significant and serious impact by disrupting the supply, communications, and economic infrastructures that support military power—impacts that could affect the daily lives of citizens across the country. In his January 2012 testimony, the Director of National Intelligence stated that, among state actors, China and Russia are of particular concern.
Phishers	Individuals or small groups execute phishing schemes in an attempt to steal identities or information for monetary gain. Phishers may also use spam and spyware or malware to accomplish their objectives.
Spammers	Individuals or organizations distribute unsolicited e-mail with hidden or false information in order to sell products, conduct phishing schemes, distribute spyware or malware, or attack organizations (e.g., a denial of service).
Spyware or malware authors	Individuals or organizations with malicious intent carry out attacks against users by producing and distributing spyware and malware. Several destructive viruses and worms have harmed files and hard drives, and reportedly have even caused physical damage to critical infrastructure, including the Melissa Macro Virus, the Explore.Zip worm, the CIH (Chernobyl) Virus, Nimda, and Code Red.
Terrorists	Terrorists seek to destroy, incapacitate, or exploit critical infrastructures in order to threaten national security, cause mass casualties, weaken the economy, and damage public morale and confidence. Terrorists may use phishing schemes or spyware/malware in order to generate funds or gather sensitive information.

Source: GAO analysis based on data from the Director of National Intelligence, Department of Justice, Central Intelligence Agency, and the Software Engineering Institute's CERT® Coordination Center.

[a]According to the Office of the National Counterintelligence Executive, industrial espionage, or theft of trade secrets, occurs when an actor, intending or knowing that his or her offense will injure the owner of a trade secret of a product produced for or placed in interstate or foreign commerce, acts with the intent to convert that trade secret to the economic benefit of anyone other than the owner. See *Foreign Spies Stealing U.S. Economic Secrets in Cyberspace*.

These sources of cybersecurity threats make use of various techniques to compromise information or adversely affect computers, software, a network, an organization's operation, an industry, or the Internet itself. Table 2 provides descriptions of common types of cyber attacks.

Table 2: Common Types of Cyber Attacks

Types of attack	Description
Cross-site scripting	An attack that uses third-party web resources to run a script within the victim's web browser or scriptable application. This occurs when a browser visits a malicious website or clicks a malicious link. The most dangerous consequences occur when this method is used to exploit additional vulnerabilities that may permit an attacker to steal cookies (data exchanged between a web server and a browser), log key strokes, capture screen shots, discover and collect network information, and remotely access and control the victim's machine.
Denial-of-service	An attack that prevents or impairs the authorized use of networks, systems, or applications by exhausting resources.
Distributed denial-of-service	A variant of the denial-of-service attack that uses numerous hosts to perform the attack.
Logic bombs	A piece of programming code intentionally inserted into a software system that will cause a malicious function to occur when one or more specified conditions are met.
Phishing	A digital form of social engineering that uses authentic-looking, but fake, e-mails to request information from users or direct them to a fake website that requests information.
Passive wiretapping	The monitoring or recording of data, such as passwords transmitted in clear text, while they are being transmitted over a communications link. This is done without altering or affecting the data.
Structured Query Language injection	An attack that involves the alteration of a database search in a web-based application, which can be used to obtain unauthorized access to sensitive information in a database.
Trojan horse	A computer program that appears to have a useful function, but also has a hidden and potentially malicious function that evades security mechanisms by, for example, masquerading as a useful program that a user would likely execute.
Virus	A computer program that can copy itself and infect a computer without the permission or knowledge of the user. A virus might corrupt or delete data on a computer, use e-mail programs to spread itself to other computers, or even erase everything on a hard disk. Unlike a worm, a virus requires human involvement (usually unwitting) to propagate.
War driving	The method of driving through cities and neighborhoods with a wireless-equipped computer–sometimes with a powerful antenna–searching for unsecured wireless networks.
Worm	A self-replicating, self-propagating, self-contained program that uses network mechanisms to spread itself. Unlike viruses, worms do not require human involvement to propagate.

Source: GAO analysis of data from the National Institute of Standards and Technology, United States Computer Emergency Readiness Team, and industry reports.

The unique nature of cyber-based attacks can vastly enhance their reach and impact, resulting in the loss of sensitive information and damage to economic and national security, the loss of privacy, identity theft, and the compromise of proprietary information or intellectual property. The increasing number of incidents reported by federal agencies, and the recently reported cyber-based attacks against individuals, businesses, critical infrastructures, and government organizations have further underscored the need to manage and bolster the cybersecurity of our government's information systems and our nation's critical infrastructures.

Number of Cyber Incidents Reported by Federal Agencies Continues to Rise

The number of cyber incidents affecting computer systems and networks continues to rise. Over the past 6 years, the number of cyber incidents reported by federal agencies to the U.S. Computer Emergency Readiness Team (US-CERT) has increased from 5,503 in fiscal year 2006 to 48,562 in fiscal year 2012, an increase of 782 percent (see fig. 1).

Figure 1: Incidents Reported to US-CERT, Fiscal Years 2006-2012

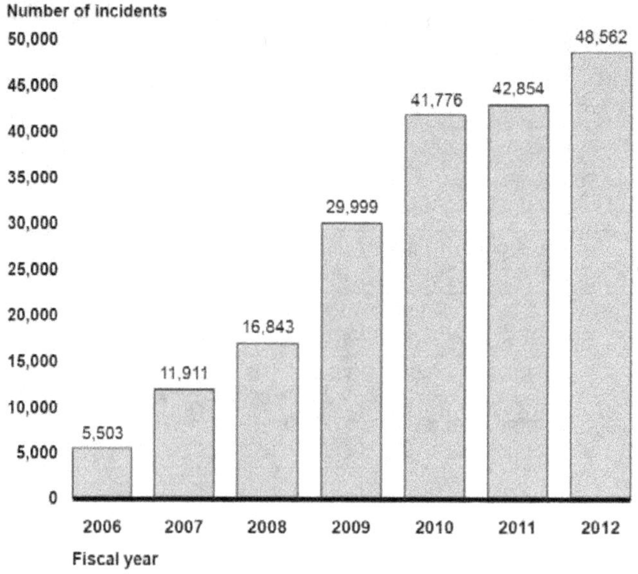

Number of incidents

Fiscal year	Number of incidents
2006	5,503
2007	11,911
2008	16,843
2009	29,999
2010	41,776
2011	42,854
2012	48,562

Fiscal year

Source: GAO analysis of US-CERT data for fiscal years 2006-2012.

Of the incidents occurring in 2012 (not including those that were reported as under investigation), improper usage,[6] malicious code, and unauthorized access were the most widely reported types across the federal government. As indicated in figure 2, which includes a breakout of incidents reported to US-CERT by agencies in fiscal year 2012, improper usage, malicious code, and unauthorized access accounted for 55 percent of total incidents reported by agencies.

---

[6]An incident is categorized as "improper usage" if a person violates acceptable computing use policies.

Figure 2: Incidents Reported to US-CERT by Federal Agencies in Fiscal Year 2012 by Category

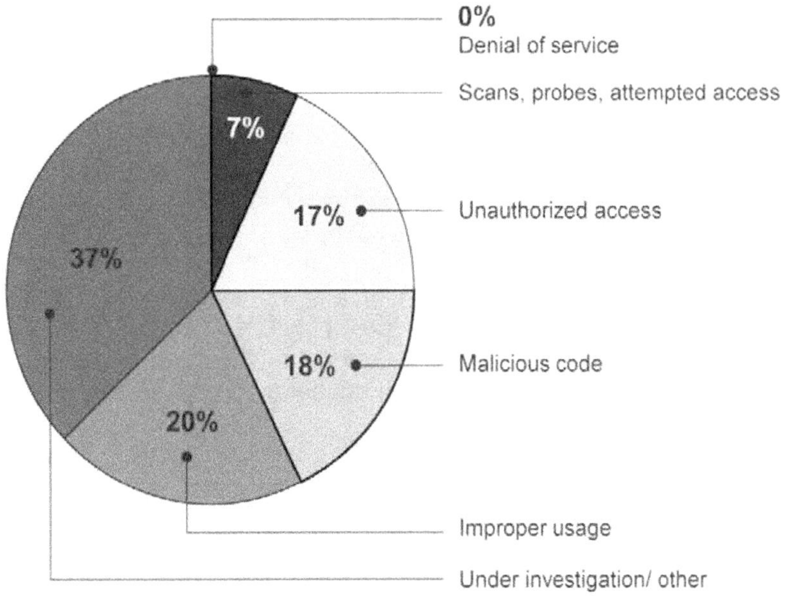

Source: GAO analysis of US-CERT data for fiscal year 2012

In addition, reports of cyber incidents affecting national security, intellectual property, and individuals have been widespread, with reported incidents involving data loss or theft, economic loss, computer intrusions, and privacy breaches. Such incidents illustrate the serious impact that cyber attacks can have on federal and military operations; critical infrastructure; and the confidentiality, integrity, and availability of sensitive government, private sector, and personal information. For example, according to US-CERT, the number of agency-reported incidents involving personally identifiable information increased 111 percent from fiscal year 2009 to fiscal year 2012—from 10,481 to 22,156.

Federal Law and Policy Establish Information Security Responsibilities for Agencies

The federal government's information security responsibilities are established in law and policy. The Federal Information Security Management Act of 2002 (FISMA)[7] sets forth a comprehensive risk-based framework for ensuring the effectiveness of information security controls over information resources that support federal operations and assets. In order to ensure the implementation of this framework, FISMA assigns specific responsibilities to agencies, the Office of Management and Budget (OMB), the National Institute of Standards and Technology (NIST), and inspectors general:

- Each agency is required to develop, document, and implement an agency-wide information security program and to report annually to OMB, selected congressional committees, and the U.S. Comptroller General on the adequacy of its information security policies, procedures, practices, and compliance with requirements.

- OMB's responsibilities include developing and overseeing the implementation of policies, principles, standards, and guidelines on information security in federal agencies (except with regard to national security systems[8]). It is also responsible for reviewing, at least annually, and approving or disapproving agency information security programs.

- NIST's responsibilities under FISMA include the development of security standards and guidelines for agencies that include standards for categorizing information and information systems according to ranges of risk levels, minimum security requirements for information and information systems in risk categories, guidelines for detection

---

[7]Title III of the E-Government Act of 2002, Pub. L. No. 107-347, Dec. 17, 2002; 44 U.S.C 3541, et seq.

[8]As defined in FISMA, the term "national security system" means any information system used by or on behalf of a federal agency that (1) involves intelligence activities, national security-related cryptologic activities, command and control of military forces, or equipment that is an integral part of a weapon or weapons system, or is critical to the direct fulfillment of military or intelligence missions (excluding systems used for routine administrative and business applications); or (2) is protected at all times by procedures established for handling classified national security information. See 44 U.S.C. § 3542(b)(2).

and handling of information security incidents, and guidelines for identifying an information system as a national security system.[9]

- Agency inspectors general are required to annually evaluate the information security program and practices of their agency. The results of these evaluations are to be submitted to OMB, and OMB is to summarize the results in its reporting to Congress.

In the 10 years since FISMA was enacted into law, executive branch oversight of agency information security has changed. As part of its FISMA oversight responsibilities, OMB has issued annual guidance to agencies on implementing FISMA requirements, including instructions for agency and inspector general reporting. However, in July 2010, the Director of OMB and the White House Cybersecurity Coordinator[10] issued a joint memorandum[11] stating that the Department of Homeland Security (DHS) was to exercise primary responsibility within the executive branch for the operational aspects of cybersecurity for federal information systems that fall within the scope of FISMA.

The OMB memo also stated that in carrying out these responsibilities, DHS is to be subject to general OMB oversight in accordance with the provisions of FISMA. In addition, the memo stated that the Cybersecurity Coordinator would lead the interagency process for cybersecurity strategy and policy development. Subsequent to the issuance of M-10-28, DHS began issuing annual reporting instructions to agencies in addition to OMB's annual guidance.

Regarding federal agencies operating national security systems, National Security Directive 42[12] established the Committee on National Security

---

[9]FISMA limits NIST to developing, in conjunction with the Department of Defense and the National Security Agency, guidelines for agencies on identifying an information system as a national security system, and for ensuring that NIST standards and guidelines are complementary with standards and guidelines developed for national security systems.

[10]In December 2009, a Special Assistant to the President was appointed as Cybersecurity Coordinator to address the recommendations made in the Obama administration's 2009 *Cyberspace Policy Review.*

[11]OMB, Memorandum M-10-28, *Clarifying Cybersecurity Responsibilities and Activities of the Executive Office of the President and the Department of Homeland Security* (Washington, D.C.: July 6, 2010).

[12]National Security Directive 42, *National Policy for the Security of National Security Telecommunications and Information Systems* (July 5, 1990).

Systems, an organization chaired by the Department of Defense (DOD), to, among other things, issue policy directives and instructions that provide mandatory information security requirements for national security systems. In addition, the defense and intelligence communities develop implementing instructions and may add additional requirements where needed. An effort is underway to harmonize policies and guidance for national security and non-national security systems. Representatives from civilian, defense, and intelligence agencies established a joint task force in 2009, led by NIST and including senior leadership and subject matter experts from participating agencies, to publish common guidance for information systems security for national security and non-national security systems.[13]

Various laws and directives have also given federal agencies responsibilities relating to the protection of critical infrastructures, which are largely owned by private sector organizations. The Homeland Security Act of 2002 created the Department of Homeland Security. Among other things, DHS was assigned with the following critical infrastructure protection responsibilities: (1) developing a comprehensive national plan for securing the critical infrastructures of the United States, (2) recommending measures to protect those critical infrastructures in coordination with other groups, and (3) disseminating, as appropriate, information to assist in the deterrence, prevention, and preemption of, or response to, terrorist attacks.

Homeland Security Presidential Directive 7 (HSPD-7) was issued in December 2003 and defined additional responsibilities for DHS, sector-specific agencies, and other departments and agencies. The directive instructed sector-specific agencies to collaborate with the private sector to identify, prioritize, and coordinate the protection of critical infrastructures to prevent, deter, and mitigate the effects of attacks. It also made DHS responsible for, among other things, coordinating national critical infrastructure protection efforts and establishing uniform policies, approaches, guidelines, and methodologies for integrating federal infrastructure protection and risk management activities within and across sectors.

---

[13]See GAO, *Information Security: Progress Made in Harmonizing Policies and Guidance for National Security and Non-National Security Systems*, GAO 10 916 (Washington, D.C.: Sept. 15, 2010).

On February 12, 2013, the President issued an executive order on improving the cybersecurity of critical infrastructure.[14] Among other things, it stated that the policy of the U.S. government is to increase the volume, timeliness, and quality of cyber threat information shared with U.S. private sector entities and ordered the following actions to be taken:

- The Attorney General, the Secretary of Homeland Security, and the Director of National Intelligence are, within 120 days of the date of the order, to issue instructions for producing unclassified reports of cyber threats and establish a process for disseminating these reports to targeted entities.
- Agencies are to coordinate their activities under the order with their senior agency officials for privacy and civil liberties and ensure that privacy and civil liberties protections are incorporated into such activities. In addition, DHS's Chief Privacy Officer and Officer for Civil Rights and Civil Liberties are to assess the privacy and civil liberties risks and recommend ways to minimize or mitigate such risks in a publicly available report to be released with 1 year of the date of the order.
- The Secretary of Homeland Security is to establish a consultative process to coordinate improvements to the cybersecurity of critical infrastructure.
- The Secretary of Commerce is to direct the Director of NIST to lead the development of a framework to reduce cyber risks to critical infrastructure. The framework is to include a set of standards, methodologies, procedures, and processes that align policy, business, and technological approaches to address cyber risks and incorporate voluntary consensus standards and industry best practices to the fullest extent possible. The Director is to publish a preliminary version of the framework within 240 days of the date of the order, and a final version within 1 year.
- The Secretary of Homeland Security, in coordination with sector-specific agencies, is to establish a voluntary program to support the adoption of the Cybersecurity Framework by owners and operators of critical infrastructure and any other interested entities. Further, the Secretary is to coordinate the establishment of a set of incentives designed to promote participation in the program and, along with the Secretaries of the Treasury and Commerce, make recommendations

---

[14]Exec. Order No. 13636, 78 Fed. Reg. 11737 (Feb. 19, 2013). The order is also available at http://www.whitehouse.gov/the-press-office/2013/02/12/executive-order-improving-critical-infrastructure-cybersecurity.

to the President that include analysis of the benefits and relative effectiveness of such incentives, and whether the incentives would require legislation or can be provided under existing law and authorities.

- The Secretary of Homeland Security, within 150 days of the date of the order, is to use a risk-based approach to identify critical infrastructure where a cybersecurity incident could reasonably result in catastrophic regional or national effects on public health or safety, economic security, or national security.

- Agencies with responsibilities for regulating the security of critical infrastructure are to consult with DHS, OMB, and the National Security Staff to review the preliminary cybersecurity framework and determine if current cybersecurity regulatory requirements are sufficient given current and projected risks. If current regulatory requirements are deemed to be insufficient, agencies are to propose actions to mitigate cyber risk, as appropriate, within 90 days of publication of the final Cybersecurity Framework. In addition, within 2 years after publication of the final framework, these agencies, in consultation with owners and operators of critical infrastructure, are to report to OMB on any critical infrastructure subject to ineffective, conflicting, or excessively burdensome cybersecurity requirements.

Also on February 12, 2013, the White House released Presidential Policy Directive (PPD) 21, on critical infrastructure security and resilience.[15] This directive revokes HSPD-7, although it states that plans developed pursuant to HSPD-7 shall remain in effect until specifically revoked or superseded. PPD-21 sets forth roles and responsibilities for DHS, sector-specific agencies, and other federal entities with regard to the protection of critical infrastructure from physical and cyber threats. It also identifies three strategic imperatives to refine and clarify functional relationships across the federal government (which includes two national critical infrastructures centers for physical and cyber infrastructure), enable efficient information exchange by identifying baseline data and systems requirements, and implement an integration and analysis function to inform planning and operational decisions.

---

[15]The White House, Presidential Policy Directive/PPD-21, *Critical Infrastructure Security and Resilience* (Feb. 12, 2013), http://www.whitehouse.gov/the-press-office/2013/02/12/presidential-policy-directive-critical-infrastructure-security-and-resil.

The directive calls for a number of specific implementation actions, along with associated time frames, which include developing a description of the functional relationships within DHS and across the federal government related to critical infrastructure security and resilience; conducting an analysis of the existing public-private partnership model; identifying baseline data and system requirements for the efficient exchange of information and intelligence; demonstrating a near real-time situational awareness capability for critical infrastructure; updating the National Infrastructure Protection Plan; and developing a national critical infrastructure security and resilience research and development plan. Finally, the directive identifies 16 critical infrastructure sectors and their designated federal sector-specific agencies.

The Federal Government Continues to Face Challenges in Effectively Implementing Cybersecurity

We and federal agency inspector general reports have identified challenges in a number of key areas of the federal government's approach to cybersecurity, including those related to protecting the nation's critical infrastructure. While actions have been taken to address aspects of these challenges, issues remain in each of the following areas.

Designing and implementing risk-based cybersecurity programs at federal agencies. Shortcomings persist in assessing risks, developing and implementing security controls, and monitoring results at federal agencies. Specifically, for fiscal year 2012, 19 of 24 major federal agencies reported that information security control deficiencies were either a material weakness or significant deficiency in internal controls over financial reporting. Further, inspectors general at 22 of 24 agencies cited information security as a major management challenge for their agency. Most of the 24 major agencies had information security weaknesses in most of five key control categories: implementing agency-wide information security management programs that are critical to identifying control deficiencies, resolving problems, and managing risks on an ongoing basis; limiting, preventing, and detecting inappropriate access to computer resources; managing the configuration of software and hardware; segregating duties to ensure that a single individual does not control all key aspects of a computer-related operation; and planning for continuity of operations in the event of a disaster or disruption (see fig. 3).

Figure 3: Information Security Weaknesses at 24 Major Agencies in Fiscal Year 2012

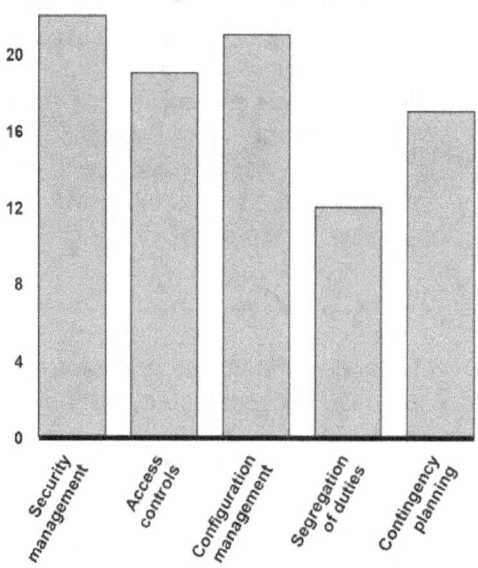

Number of agencies

Information security weaknesses

Source: GAO analysis of agency, inspectors general, and GAO reports as of December 13, 2012.

As we noted in our October 2011 report on agencies' implementation of FISMA requirements, an underlying reason for these weaknesses is that agencies have not fully implemented their information security programs.[16] As a result, they have limited assurance that controls are in place and operating as intended to protect their information resources, thereby leaving them vulnerable to attack or compromise. Accordingly, we have continued to make numerous recommendations to address specific weaknesses in risk management processes at individual federal agencies. Recently, some agencies have demonstrated improvement in this area. For example, we reported in November 2012 that during fiscal year 2012, the Internal Revenue Service (IRS) continued to make important progress in addressing numerous deficiencies in its information

---

[16]GAO, *Information Security: Weaknesses Continue Amid New Federal Efforts to Implement Requirements*, GAO-12-137 (Washington, D.C.: Oct. 3, 2011).

security controls over its financial reporting systems.[17] Nonetheless, applying effective controls over agency information and information systems remains an area of significant concern.

Establishing and identifying standards for critical infrastructures. As we reported in December 2011, DHS and other agencies with responsibilities for specific critical infrastructure sectors have not yet identified cybersecurity guidance applicable to or widely used in each of the sectors.[18] Moreover, sectors vary in the extent to which they are required by law or regulation to comply with specific cybersecurity requirements. Within the energy sector, for example, experts have identified a lack of clarity in the division of responsibility between federal and state regulators as a challenge in securing the U.S. electricity grid. We have made recommendations aimed at furthering efforts by sector-specific agencies to enhance critical infrastructure protection. The recently issued executive order is also intended to bolster efforts in this challenge area.

Detecting, responding to, and mitigating cyber incidents. DHS has made progress in coordinating the federal response to cyber incidents, but challenges remain in sharing information among federal agencies and key private-sector entities, including critical infrastructure owners. Difficulties in sharing information and the lack of a centralized information-sharing system continue to hinder progress. The February executive order contains provisions aimed at addressing these difficulties by, for example, establishing a process for disseminating unclassified reports of threat information. Challenges also persist in developing a timely cyber analysis and warning capability. While DHS has taken steps to establish a timely analysis and warning capability, we have reported that it had yet to establish a predictive analysis capability and recommended that the department establish such capabilities.[19] According to DHS, tools for predictive analysis are to be tested in fiscal year 2013.

---

[17]GAO, *Financial Audit: IRS's Fiscal Years 2012 and 2011 Financial Statements*, GAO-13-120 (Washington, D.C.: Nov. 9, 2012).

[18]GAO, *Critical Infrastructure Protection: Cybersecurity Guidance Is Available, but More Can Be Done to Promote Its Use*, GAO-12-92 (Washington, D.C.: Dec. 9, 2011).

[19]GAO, *Cyber Analysis and Warning: DHS Faces Challenges in Establishing a Comprehensive National Capability*, GAO-08-588 (Washington, D.C.: July 31, 2008).

Promoting education, awareness, and workforce planning. In November 2011, we reported that federal agencies leading strategic planning efforts for cybersecurity education and awareness had not identified details for achieving planned outcomes and that specific tasks and responsibilities were unclear.[20] We recommended, among other things, that these agencies collaborate to clarify responsibilities and processes for planning and monitoring their activities. We also reported that only two of eight agencies in our review had developed cyber workforce plans, and only three of the eight agencies had a department-wide training program for their cybersecurity workforce. We recommended that these agencies take steps to improve agency and government-wide cybersecurity workforce efforts. Agencies concurred with the majority of our recommendations and outlined steps to address them.

Supporting cyber research and development. The support of targeted cyber research and development (R&D) has been impeded by implementation challenges among federal agencies. In June 2010, we reported that R&D initiatives were hindered by limited sharing of detailed information about ongoing research, including the lack of a process for sharing results of completed projects or a repository to track R&D projects funded by the federal government.[21] To help facilitate information sharing about planned and ongoing R&D projects, we recommended establishing a mechanism for tracking ongoing and completed federal cybersecurity R&D projects and their funding, and that this mechanism be used to develop an ongoing process to share R&D information among federal agencies and the private sector. As of September 2012, this mechanism had not been fully developed.

Securing the use of new technologies. Addressing security concerns related to the use of emerging technologies such as cloud computing, social media, and mobile devices is a continuing challenge. In May 2010, we reported that federal agencies had not taken adequate steps to ensure that security concerns were addressed in their use of cloud-based services, and made several recommendations to address cloud

---

[20]GAO, *Cybersecurity Human Capital: Initiatives Need Better Planning and Coordination*, GAO-12-8 (Washington, D.C.: Nov. 29, 2011).

[21]GAO, *Cybersecurity: Key Challenges Need to Be Addressed to Improve Research and Development*, GAO-10-466 (June 3, 2010).

computing security, which agencies have begun to implement.[22] Further, we reported in June 2011 that federal agencies did not always have adequate policies in place for managing and protecting information they access and disseminate through social media platforms such as Facebook and Twitter and recommended that agencies develop such policies.[23] Most of the agencies agreed with our recommendations. In September 2012, we reported that the U.S. Federal Communications Commission could do more to encourage mobile device manufacturers and wireless carriers to implement a more complete industry baseline of mobile security safeguards.[24] The commission generally concurred with our recommendations.

Managing risks to the global information technology supply chain.
Reliance on a global supply chain for information technology products and services introduces risks to systems, and federal agencies have not always addressed these risks. Specifically, in March 2012, we reported that four national security-related agencies varied in the extent to which they had defined supply chain protection measures for their information systems and were not in a position to develop implementing procedures and monitoring capabilities for such measures.[25] We recommended that the agencies take steps as needed to address supply chain risks, and the departments generally concurred.

Addressing international cybersecurity challenges. While the federal government has identified the importance of international cooperation for cybersecurity and has assigned related roles and responsibilities to federal agencies, its approach to addressing international aspects of cybersecurity has not been fully defined or implemented. We reported in July 2010 that the government faced a number of challenges in this area, relating to providing top-level leadership to coordinate actions among

---

[22]GAO, *Information Security: Federal Guidance Needed to Address Control Issues with Implementing Cloud Computing*, GAO-10-513 (Washington, D.C.: May 27, 2010).

[23]GAO, *Social Media: Federal Agencies Need Policies and Procedures for Managing and Protecting Information They Access and Disseminate*, GAO-11-605 (Washington, D.C.: June 28, 2011).

[24]GAO, *Information Security: Better Implementation of Controls for Mobile Devices Should Be Encouraged*, GAO-12-757 (Washington, D.C.: Sept. 18, 2012).

[25]GAO, *IT Supply Chain: National Security-Related Agencies Need to Better Address Risks*, GAO-12-361 (Washington, D.C.: Mar. 23, 2012).

agencies, developing a national strategy, coordinating policy among key federal entities, ensuring that international technical standards and policies do not impose unnecessary trade barriers, participating in international cyber-incident response efforts, investigating and prosecuting international cybercrime, and developing international models and norms for behavior.[26] We recommended that the government develop a global cyberspace strategy to help address these challenges. While such a strategy has been developed and includes goals such as the development of international cyberspace norms, it does not fully specify outcome-oriented performance metrics or timeframes for completing activities.

The U.S. National Cybersecurity Strategy Has Evolved over Time but Is Not Well Defined

The federal government has issued a variety of documents over the last decade that were intended to articulate a national cybersecurity strategy. The evolution of the nation's cybersecurity strategy is summarized in figure 4.

---

[26]GAO, *Cyberspace: United States Faces Challenges in Addressing Global Cybersecurity and Governance*, GAO-10-606 (Washington, D.C.: July 2, 2010).

Figure 4: Evolution of National Strategies Related to Cybersecurity

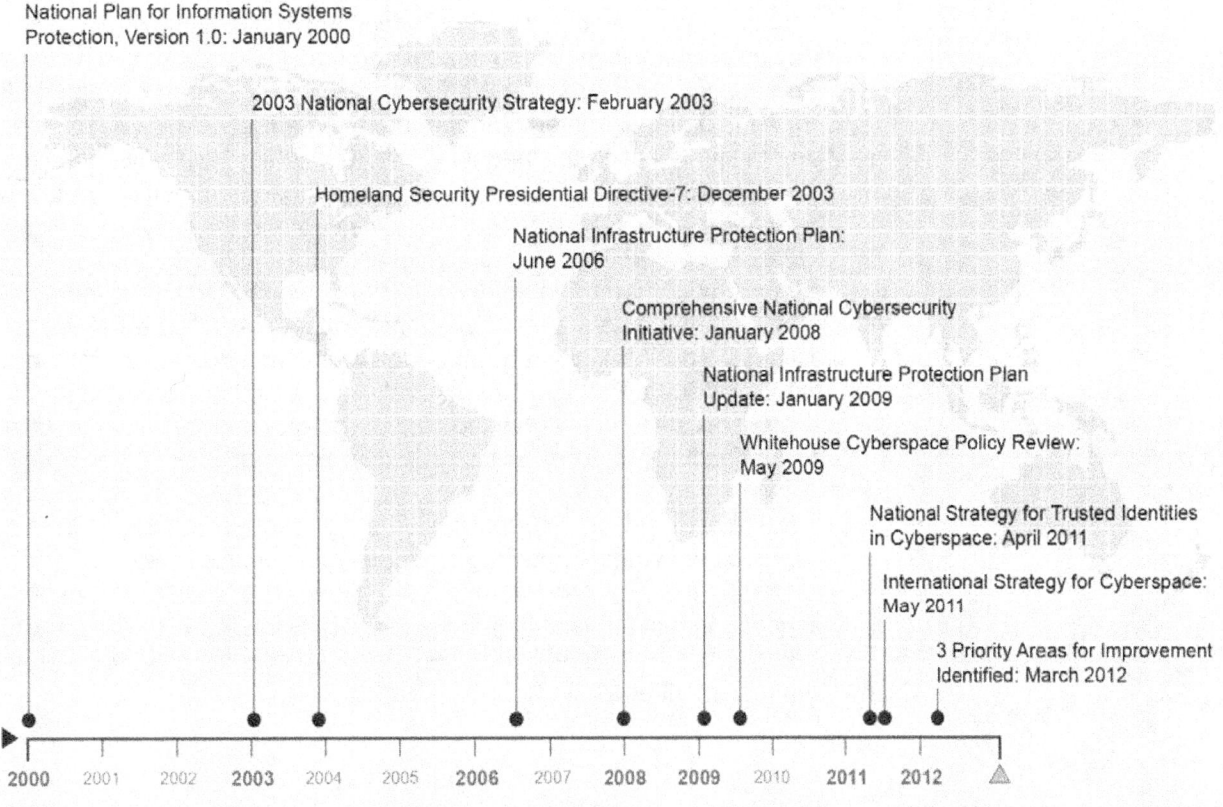

National Plan for Information Systems
Protection, Version 1.0: January 2000

2003 National Cybersecurity Strategy: February 2003

Homeland Security Presidential Directive-7: December 2003

National Infrastructure Protection Plan:
June 2006

Comprehensive National Cybersecurity
Initiative: January 2008

National Infrastructure Protection Plan
Update: January 2009

Whitehouse Cyberspace Policy Review:
May 2009

National Strategy for Trusted Identities
in Cyberspace: April 2011

International Strategy for Cyberspace:
May 2011

3 Priority Areas for Improvement
Identified: March 2012

2000　2001　2002　2003　2004　2005　2006　2007　2008　2009　2010　2011　2012

Source. GAO analysis of federal strategy documents.

These strategy documents address aspects of the above-mentioned challenge areas. For example, they address priorities for enhancing cybersecurity within the federal government as well as for encouraging improvements in the cybersecurity of critical infrastructures within the private sector.

However, as we noted in our February 2013 report, the government has not developed an overarching national cybersecurity strategy that synthesizes the relevant portions of these documents or provides a comprehensive description of the current strategy.[27] The Obama administration's 2009 *Cyberspace Policy Review* recommended a number of actions, including updating the 2003 *National Cybersecurity Strategy*. However, no updated strategy document has been issued. In May 2011, the White House announced that it had completed all the near-term actions outlined in the 2009 policy review, including the update to the 2003 national strategy. According to the administration's fact sheet on cybersecurity accomplishments,[28] the 2009 policy review itself serves as the updated strategy. The fact sheet stated that the direction and needs highlighted in the *Cyberspace Policy Review* and the previous national cybersecurity strategy were still relevant, and it noted that the administration had updated its strategy on two subordinate cyber issues, identity management and international engagement. Nonetheless, these actions do not fulfill the recommendation that an updated strategy be prepared for the President's approval. As a result, no overarching strategy exists to show how the various goals and activities articulated in current documents form an integrated strategic approach.

In addition to lacking an integrated strategy, the government's current approach to cybersecurity lacks key desirable characteristics of a national strategy. In 2004, we developed a set of desirable characteristics that can enhance the usefulness of national strategies in allocating resources, defining policies, and helping to ensure accountability.[29] Table 3 summarizes these key desirable characteristics.

---

[27]GAO-13-187.

[28]The White House, "Fact Sheet: The Administration's Cybersecurity Accomplishments" (May 12, 2011), accessed on July 26, 2012, http://www.whitehouse.gov/the-press-office/2011/05/12/fact-sheet-administrations-cybersecurity-accomplishments.

[29]See GAO, *Combating Terrorism: Evaluation of Selected Characteristics in National Strategies Related to Terrorism*, GAO-04-408T (Washington, D.C.: Feb. 3, 2004).

Table 3: Desirable Characteristics for a National Strategy

Desirable characteristic	Description
Purpose, scope, and methodology	Addresses why the strategy was produced, the scope of its coverage, and the process by which it was developed.
Problem definition and risk assessment	Addresses the particular national problems and threats the strategy is directed toward.
Goals, subordinate objectives, activities, and performance measures	Addresses what the strategy is trying to achieve and steps to achieve those results, as well as the priorities, milestones, and performance measures to gauge results.
Resources, investments, and risk management	Addresses what implementation of the strategy will cost, the sources and types of resources and investments needed, and where resources and investments should be targeted based on balancing risk reductions with costs.
Organizational roles, responsibilities, and coordination	Addresses who will be implementing the strategy, what their roles will be compared to others, and mechanisms for them to coordinate their efforts.
Linkage to other strategies and implementation	Addresses how a national strategy relates to other strategies' goals, objectives, and activities, and to subordinate levels of government and their plans to implement the strategy.

Source: GAO.

Existing cybersecurity strategy documents have included selected elements of these desirable characteristics, such as setting goals and subordinate objectives, but have generally lacked other key elements. The missing elements include the following:

Milestones and performance measures. The government's strategy documents include few milestones or performance measures, making it difficult to track progress in accomplishing stated goals and objectives. This lack of milestones and performance measures at the strategic level is mirrored in similar shortcomings within key programs that are part of the government-wide strategy. For example, in 2011 the DHS inspector general recommended that the department develop and implement performance measures to track and evaluate the effectiveness of actions defined in its strategic plan,[30] which the department had yet to do as of January 2012.

Cost and resources. While past strategy documents linked certain activities to federal agency budget requests, none have fully addressed cost and resources, including justifying the required investment, which is critical to gaining support for implementation. Specifically, none of the

---

[30]DHS, Office of Inspector General, *Planning, Management, and Systems Issues Hinder DHS' Efforts to Protect Cyberspace and the Nation's Cyber Infrastructure*, OIG-11-89 (Washington, D.C.: June 2011).

strategy documents provided full assessments of anticipated costs and how resources might be allocated to meet them.

Roles and responsibilities. Cybersecurity strategy documents have assigned high-level roles and responsibilities but have left important details unclear. Several GAO reports have likewise demonstrated that the roles and responsibilities of key agencies charged with protecting the cyber assets of the United States are inadequately defined. For example, the chartering directives for several offices within the Department of Defense assign overlapping roles and responsibilities for preparing for and responding to domestic cyber incidents. In an October 2012 report, we recommended that the department update its guidance on preparing for and responding to domestic cyber incidents to include a description of roles and responsibilities.[31] Further, in March 2010, we reported that agencies had overlapping and uncoordinated responsibilities within the Comprehensive National Cybersecurity Initiative and recommended that OMB better define roles and responsibilities for all key participants.[32]

In addition, while the law gives OMB responsibility for oversight of federal information security, OMB transferred several of its oversight responsibilities to DHS. OMB officials stated that enlisting DHS to perform these responsibilities has allowed OMB to have more visibility into agencies' cybersecurity activities because of the additional resources and expertise provided by DHS. While OMB's decision to transfer these responsibilities is not consistent with FISMA, it may have had beneficial practical results, such as leveraging resources from DHS. Nonetheless, with these responsibilities now divided between the two organizations, it is remains unclear how they are to share oversight of individual departments and agencies. Additional legislation could clarify these responsibilities.

Linkage with other key strategy documents. Existing cybersecurity strategy documents vary in terms of priorities and structure, and do not specify how they link to or supersede other documents. Nor do they

---

[31]GAO, *Homeland Defense: DOD Needs to Address Gaps in Homeland Defense and Civil Support Guidance*, GAO-13-128 (Washington, D.C.: Oct. 24, 2012).

[32]GAO, *Cybersecurity: Progress Made but Challenges Remain in Defining and Coordinating the Comprehensive National Initiative*, GAO-10-338 (Washington, D.C.: Mar. 5, 2010).

describe how they fit into an overarching national cybersecurity strategy. For example, in 2012, the Obama administration identified three cross-agency cybersecurity priorities, but no explanation was given as to how these priorities related to those established in other strategy documents.

Actions Needed to Ensure More Effective Implementation of Cybersecurity

Given the range and sophistication of the threats and potential exploits that confront government agencies and the nation's cyber critical infrastructure, it is critical that the government adopt a comprehensive strategic approach to mitigating the risks of successful cybersecurity attacks. In our February report, we recommended that the White House Cybersecurity Coordinator develop an overarching federal cybersecurity strategy that includes all key elements of the desirable characteristics of a national strategy.[33] Such a strategy, we believe, will provide a more effective framework for implementing cybersecurity activities and better ensure that such activities will lead to progress in securing systems and information. This strategy should also better ensure that federal government departments and agencies are held accountable for making significant improvements in cybersecurity challenge areas by, among other things, clarifying how oversight will be carried out by OMB and other federal entities. In the absence of such an integrated strategy, the documents that comprise the government's current strategic approach are of limited value as a tool for mobilizing actions to mitigate the most serious threats facing the nation.

In addition, many of the recommendations previously made by us and agency inspectors general have not yet been fully addressed, leaving much room for more progress in addressing cybersecurity challenges. In many cases, the causes of these challenges are closely related to the key elements that are missing from the government's cybersecurity strategy. For example, the persistence of shortcomings in agency cybersecurity risk management processes indicates that agencies have not been held accountable for effectively implementing such processes and that oversight mechanisms have not been clear. It is just such oversight and accountability that is poorly defined in cybersecurity strategy documents.

In light of this limited oversight and accountability, we also stated in our report that Congress should consider legislation to better define roles and

---

[33]GAO-13-187.

responsibilities for implementing and overseeing federal information security programs and protecting the nation's critical cyber assets. Such legislation could clarify the respective responsibilities of OMB and DHS, as well as those of other key federal departments and agencies.

In commenting on a draft of the report, the Executive Office of the President agreed that more needs to be done to develop a coherent and comprehensive strategy on cybersecurity but did not believe producing another strategy document would be beneficial. Specifically, the office stated that remaining flexible and focusing on achieving measurable improvements in cybersecurity would be more beneficial than developing "yet another strategy on top of existing strategies." We agree that flexibility and a focus on achieving measurable improvements in cybersecurity is critically important and that simply preparing another document, if not integrated with previous documents, would not be helpful. The focus of our recommendation is to develop an overarching strategy that integrates the numerous strategy documents, establishes milestones and performance measures, and better ensures that federal departments and agencies are held accountable for making significant improvements in cybersecurity challenge areas. The Executive Office of the President also agreed that Congress should consider enhanced cybersecurity legislation that addresses information sharing and baseline standards for critical infrastructure, among other things.

In summary, addressing the ongoing challenges in implementing effective cybersecurity within the government, as well as in collaboration with the private sector and other partners, requires the federal government to define and implement a coherent and comprehensive national strategy that includes key desirable elements and provides accountability for results. Recent efforts, such as the 2012 cross-agency priorities and the executive order on improving cybersecurity for critical infrastructure, could provide parts of a strategic approach. For example, the executive order includes actions aimed at addressing challenges in developing standards for critical infrastructure and sharing information, in addition to assigning specific responsibilities to specific individuals that are to be completed within specific timeframes, thus providing clarity of responsibility and a means for establishing accountability. However, these efforts need to be integrated into an overarching strategy that includes a clearer process for oversight of agency risk management and a roadmap for improving the cybersecurity challenge areas in order for the government to make significant progress in furthering its strategic goals and lessening persistent weaknesses.

Chairmen Rockefeller and Carper, Ranking Members Thune and Coburn, and Members of the Committees, this concludes my statement. I would be happy to answer any questions you may have.

GAO Contacts and Acknowledgments

If you have any questions regarding this statement, please contact Gregory C. Wilshusen at (202) 512-6244 or wilshuseng@gao.gov or Dr. Nabajyoti Barkakati at (202) 512-4499 or barkakatin@gao.gov. Other key contributors to this statement include John de Ferrari (Assistant Director), Richard B. Hung (Assistant Director), Nicole Jarvis, Lee McCracken, David F. Plocher, and Jeffrey Woodward.

Appendix I: Related GAO Products

Cybersecurity: National Strategy, Roles, and Responsibilities Need to Be Better Defined and More Effectively Implemented. GAO-13-187. Washington, D.C.: February 14, 2013.

High-Risk Series: An Update. GAO-13-283. Washington, D.C.: February 14, 2013.

Information Security: Federal Communications Commission Needs to Strengthen Controls over Enhanced Secured Network Project. GAO-13-155. Washington, D.C.: January 25, 2013.

Information Security: Actions Needed by Census Bureau to Address Weaknesses. GAO-13-63. Washington, D.C.: January 22, 2013.

Information Security: Better Implementation of Controls for Mobile Devices Should Be Encouraged. GAO-12-757. Washington, D.C.: September 18, 2012.

Mobile Device Location Data: Additional Federal Actions Could Help Protect Consumer Privacy. GAO-12-903. Washington, D.C.: September 11, 2012.

Medical Devices: FDA Should Expand Its Consideration of Information Security for Certain Types of Devices. GAO-12-816. August 31, 2012.

Cybersecurity: Challenges in Securing the Electricity Grid. GAO-12-926T. Washington, D.C.: July 17, 2012.

Electronic Warfare: DOD Actions Needed to Strengthen Management and Oversight. GAO-12-479. Washington, D.C.: July 9, 2012.

Information Security: Cyber Threats Facilitate Ability to Commit Economic Espionage. GAO-12-876T. Washington, D.C.: June 28, 2012.

Cybersecurity: Threats Impacting the Nation. GAO-12-666T. Washington, D.C.: April 24, 2012.

IT Supply Chain: National Security-Related Agencies Need to Better Address Risks. GAO-12-361. Washington, D.C.: March 23, 2012.

Information Security: IRS Needs to Further Enhance Internal Control over Financial Reporting and Taxpayer Data. GAO-12-393. Washington, D.C.: March 16, 2012.

Cybersecurity: Challenges in Securing the Modernized Electricity Grid. GAO-12-507T. Washington, D.C.: February 28, 2012.

Critical Infrastructure Protection: Cybersecurity Guidance Is Available, but More Can Be Done to Promote Its Use. GAO-12-92. Washington, D.C.: December 9, 2011.

Cybersecurity Human Capital: Initiatives Need Better Planning and Coordination. GAO-12-8. Washington, D.C.: November 29, 2011.

Information Security: Additional Guidance Needed to Address Cloud Computing Concerns. GAO-12-130T. Washington, D.C.: October 6, 2011.

Information Security: Weaknesses Continue Amid New Federal Efforts to Implement Requirements. GAO-12-137. Washington, D.C.: October 3, 2011.

Personal ID Verification: Agencies Should Set a Higher Priority on Using the Capabilities of Standardized Identification Cards. GAO-11-751. Washington, D.C.: September 20, 2011.

Information Security: FDIC Has Made Progress, but Further Actions Are Needed to Protect Financial Data. GAO-11-708. Washington, D.C.: August 12, 2011.

Cybersecurity: Continued Attention Needed to Protect Our Nation's Critical Infrastructure. GAO-11-865T. Washington, D.C.: July 26, 2011.

Defense Department Cyber Efforts: DOD Faces Challenges in Its Cyber Activities. GAO-11-75. Washington, D.C.: July 25, 2011.

Information Security: State Has Taken Steps to Implement a Continuous Monitoring Application, but Key Challenges Remain. GAO-11-149. Washington, D.C.: July 8, 2011.

Social Media: Federal Agencies Need Policies and Procedures for Managing and Protecting Information They Access and Disseminate. GAO-11-605. Washington, D.C.: June 28, 2011.

Cybersecurity: Continued Attention Needed to Protect Our Nation's Critical Infrastructure and Federal Information Systems. GAO-11-463T. Washington, D.C.: March 16, 2011.

Information Security: IRS Needs to Enhance Internal Control Over Financial Reporting and Taxpayer Data. GAO-11-308. Washington, D.C.: March 15, 2011.

Electricity Grid Modernization: Progress Being Made on Cybersecurity Guidelines, but Key Challenges Remain to Be Addressed. GAO-11-117. Washington, D.C.: January 12, 2011.

Information Security: National Nuclear Security Administration Needs to Improve Contingency Planning for Its Classified Supercomputing Operations. GAO-11-67. Washington, D.C.: December 9, 2010.

Information Security: Federal Agencies Have Taken Steps to Secure Wireless Networks, but Further Actions Can Mitigate Risk. GAO-11-43. Washington, D.C.: November 30, 2010.

Information Security: Federal Deposit Insurance Corporation Needs to Mitigate Control Weaknesses. GAO-11-29. Washington, D.C.: November 30, 2010.

Information Security: National Archives and Records Administration Needs to Implement Key Program Elements and Controls. GAO-11-20. Washington, D.C.: October 21, 2010.

Cyberspace Policy: Executive Branch Is Making Progress Implementing 2009 Policy Review Recommendations, but Sustained Leadership Is Needed. GAO-11-24. Washington, D.C.: October 6, 2010.

Information Security: Progress Made on Harmonizing Policies and Guidance for National Security and Non-National Security Systems. GAO-10-916. Washington, D.C.: September 15, 2010.

Information Management: Challenges in Federal Agencies' Use of Web 2.0 Technologies. GAO-10-872T. Washington, D.C.: July 22, 2010.

Critical Infrastructure Protection: Key Private and Public Cyber Expectations Need to Be Consistently Addressed. GAO-10-628. Washington, D.C.: July 15, 2010.

Cyberspace: United States Faces Challenges in Addressing Global Cybersecurity and Governance. GAO-10-606. Washington, D.C.: July 2, 2010.

Information Security: Governmentwide Guidance Needed to Assist Agencies in Implementing Cloud Computing. GAO-10-855T. Washington, D.C.: July 1, 2010.

Cybersecurity: Continued Attention Is Needed to Protect Federal Information Systems from Evolving Threats. GAO-10-834T. Washington, D.C.: June 16, 2010.

Cybersecurity: Key Challenges Need to Be Addressed to Improve Research and Development. GAO-10-466. Washington, D.C.: June 3, 2010.

Information Security: Federal Guidance Needed to Address Control Issues with Implementing Cloud Computing. GAO-10-513. Washington, D.C.: May 27, 2010.

Information Security: Opportunities Exist for the Federal Housing Finance Agency to Improve Control. GAO-10-528. Washington, D.C.: April 30, 2010.

Information Security: Concerted Response Needed to Resolve Persistent Weaknesses. GAO-10-536T.Washington, D.C.: March 24, 2010.

Information Security: IRS Needs to Continue to Address Significant Weaknesses. GAO-10-355. Washington, D.C.: March 19, 2010.

Information Security: Concerted Effort Needed to Consolidate and Secure Internet Connections at Federal Agencies. GAO-10-237. Washington, D.C.: March 12, 2010.

Information Security: Agencies Need to Implement Federal Desktop Core Configuration Requirements. GAO-10-202. Washington, D.C.: March 12, 2010.

Cybersecurity: Progress Made but Challenges Remain in Defining and Coordinating the Comprehensive National Initiative. GAO-10-338. Washington, D.C.: March 5, 2010.

Critical Infrastructure Protection: Update to National Infrastructure Protection Plan Includes Increased Emphasis on Risk Management and Resilience. GAO-10-296. Washington, D.C.: March 5, 2010.

Department of Veterans Affairs' Implementation of Information Security Education Assistance Program. GAO-10-170R. Washington, D.C.: December 18, 2009.

Cybersecurity: Continued Efforts Are Needed to Protect Information Systems from Evolving Threats. GAO-10-230T. Washington, D.C.: November 17, 2009.

Information Security: Concerted Effort Needed to Improve Federal Performance Measures. GAO-10-159T. Washington, D.C.: October 29, 2009.

Critical Infrastructure Protection: OMB Leadership Needed to Strengthen Agency Planning Efforts to Protect Federal Cyber Assets. GAO-10-148. Washington, D.C.: October 15, 2009.

Information Security: NASA Needs to Remedy Vulnerabilities in Key Networks. GAO-10-4. Washington, D.C.: October 15, 2009.

Information Security: Actions Needed to Better Manage, Protect, and Sustain Improvements to Los Alamos National Laboratory's Classified Computer Network. GAO-10-28. Washington, D.C.: October 14, 2009.

Critical Infrastructure Protection: Current Cyber Sector-Specific Planning Approach Needs Reassessment. GAO-09-969. Washington, D.C.: September 24, 2009.

Information Security: Federal Information Security Issues. GAO-09-817R. Washington, D.C.: June 30, 2009.

Information Security: Concerted Effort Needed to Improve Federal Performance Measures. GAO-09-617. Washington, D.C.: September 14, 2009.

Information Security: Agencies Continue to Report Progress, but Need to Mitigate Persistent Weaknesses. GAO-09-546. Washington, D.C.: July 17, 2009.

National Cybersecurity Strategy: Key Improvements Are Needed to Strengthen the Nation's Posture. GAO-09-432T. Washington, D.C.: March 10, 2009.

Information Technology: Federal Laws, Regulations, and Mandatory Standards to Securing Private Sector Information Technology Systems and Data in Critical Infrastructure Sectors. GAO-08-1075R. Washington, D.C.: September 16, 2008.

Cyber Analysis and Warning: DHS Faces Challenges in Establishing a Comprehensive National Capability. GAO-08-588. Washington, D.C.: July 31, 2008.

Information Security: Federal Agency Efforts to Encrypt Sensitive Information Are Under Way, but Work Remains. GAO-08-525. Washington, D.C.: June 27, 2008.

Privacy: Lessons Learned about Data Breach Notification. GAO-07-657. Washington, D.C.: April 30, 2007.